The 2.4 mile (4 km) long Parsenn Railway in Switzerland is operated in two sections and uses cars coupled in pairs. On longer funicular lines it becomes necessary to split the line into sections, with an intermediate change of car, in order to increase capacity and to overcome the problems associated with a single, very long cable.

FUNICULAR RAILWAYS

John Woodhams

Shire Publications Ltd

CONTENTS

The funicular principle 3

The inclined plane 5

Cliff railways 11

Cable tramways 27

Further reading 32

Places to visit 32

 First published 1989. Shire Album 240. ISBN 0 7478 0040 5.

Printed in Great Britain by C. I. Thomas & Sons (Haverfordwest) Ltd, Press Buildings, Merlins Bridge, Haverfordwest, Dyfed SA61 1XF.

British Library Cataloguing in Publication Data: Woodhams, John. Funicular railways. 1. Funicular services, history. I. Title. 385'6. ISBN 0-7478-0040-5.

ACKNOWLEDGEMENTS
Illustrations are acknowledged as follows: Bradford Trolleybus Association, page 30 (both); British Waterways Board, page 5 (top); Cleveland County Council, page 11; E. Course, page 12 (top left); G. Emerson, page 8 (top); L. Folkard, page 19; J. Furness, pages 8 (bottom), 9 (both); M. Hoather, pages 12 (top right and bottom), 21 (bottom left); Ironbridge Gorge Museum Trust, page 4; A. A. Jackson, page 25 (bottom); M. Lane, pages 2, 15 (top); J. H. Meredith, pages 10 (bottom), 13 (top), 14 (top), 15 (bottom), 16 (both), 17 (both), 18 (both), 20 (both), 21 (bottom right), 22, 23 (both), 24; C. E. Mountford Collection, page 7 (both); Swiss National Tourist Office, page 1; J. Webb, page 27; D. W. Winkworth, pages 25 (top), 26 (both); John Woodhams, pages 10 (top), 13 (lower three), 14 (bottom), 28 (both), 29 (both), 31, and front cover; John Woodhams Collection, pages 3, 5 (bottom), 21 (top).

Cover: *The East Hill Lift at Hastings, East Sussex, was built by the local authority in 1903. The two cars are about to pass at the midpoint of the line.*

Below: *The four-track Clifton Rocks Railway in Bristol was built entirely in tunnel and was worked as two separate double-track counterbalanced lines.*

The 2¼ mile (3.6 km) line to the summit of the Stanserhorn in Switzerland is worked in three sections. A stepped-floor car is seen here on the lower slopes.

THE FUNICULAR PRINCIPLE

Conventional railways, relying upon the principle of steel wheel on smooth steel rail for adhesion, have always been limited by the maximum gradients possible for locomotive operation. Several methods have been adopted to overcome this handicap, including cable haulage and rack and pinion traction, the latter involving a toothed wheel on the axle of a locomotive engaging in a rack located between the running rails.

The term 'funicular railway' often conjures visions of the little cliff railways that may be found at a number of seaside resorts. However, 'funicular' is defined as 'of a rope or its tension': it covers all forms of railway and tramway worked by a cable system of haulage and not only steeply graded lines.

There exist medieval engravings of carts being hauled by cable up steep gradients. Following the industrial revolution, wagonways sometimes incorporated a steep incline, along which wagons were rope-hauled by a horse-gin.

In 1750 Michael Menzies, a Scottish advocate, patented the self-acting inclined plane. This utilised a double track and operated on the principle that loaded wagons descending on one line can be used to raise empty or partly laden wagons on the adjacent track. The idea of adding an external power source was then developed: initially horse-gins but later a stationary steam engine. The principle of counterbalancing ascending and descending wagons was still maintained to minimise the additional power required.

An alternative idea, if a suitable supply could be made available, was to use water instead of animal or steam power. This could be achieved by the installation of a waterwheel to power a winding-drum, or by fitting the rail vehicles with water tanks which could be filled before the downward journey and emptied at the lower station before the return ascent. This water-balance idea was a development of the self-acting incline and required a double-track railway with each vehicle, or group of vehicles, moving in one direction to be counterbalanced by a corresponding train travelling at exactly the same time in the opposite direction.

In recent years a number of funiculars originally built for steam or hydraulic operation have been rebuilt with electric winding-gear.

With all these systems the vehicles themselves are not driven in the conventional sense, the centre of operations being the winding-house. The driver is really a brakesman, who is able to stop the car if necessary. Moreover, in any 'balanced' system, where cars or wagons are attached to a common cable, neither can move until both ascending and descending trains are ready.

The Hay inclined plane is now preserved at the Blists Hill Museum site, part of the Ironbridge Gorge complex, Shropshire. This view dates from the late nineteenth century.

This view of the Trench inclined plane clearly shows an example of the wheeled trolley on to which boats were loaded. Note that the undercarriage is built so that the boat is carried in a horizontal position.

THE INCLINED PLANE

The problem of gradients was even more apparent to the canal builders: boats were normally raised and lowered between different levels by means of locks.

However, in very hilly country the inclined plane was used to eliminate the need for long flights of locks, which would be costly in their use of water. This inclined plane was essentially a funicular railway built between two levels of canal, by which boats were carried in caissons on wheeled underframes. The body of the caisson was kept level, on an irregularly shaped chassis, to compensate for the gradient of the plane. Boats were usually loaded and unloaded in locks at each end.

The first such plane in England was on the Ketley Canal in Shropshire, built by William Reynolds in 1788, with a rise of 73 feet (22 metres). Here boatloads of iron ore were lowered from the main canal to Ketley ironworks, so that descending laden boats counterbalanced ascending empty or partly laden boats on the double-track incline.

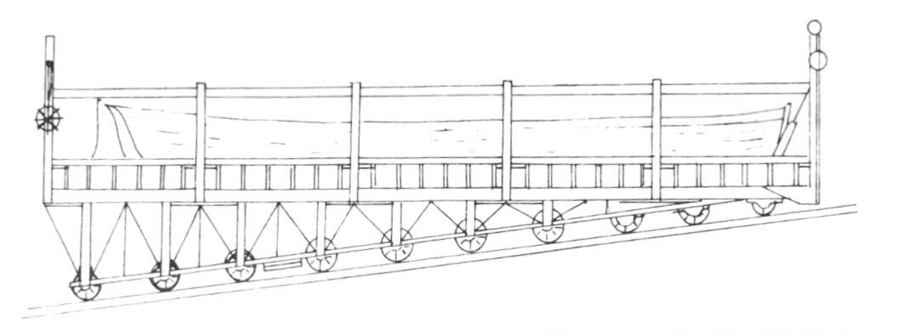

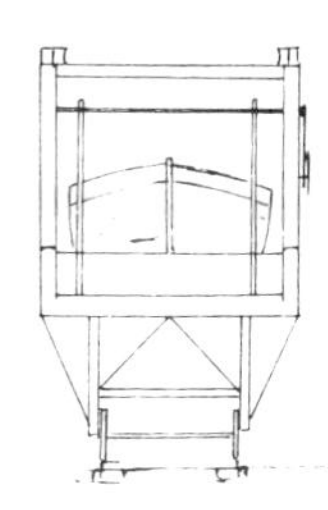

This large vehicle was used for the carriage of boats on the Blackhill plane of the Monkland Canal.

About twenty inclined planes were constructed on the canal network, many using a steam winding-engine and others a waterwheel. An unusual mechanism was constructed on the Bude Canal at Hobbacott Down, Cornwall. Two wells were sunk at the top of the double-track incline and a boat was raised by means of a large container full of water descending one of the well shafts. As the boat reached the top of the climb the water could be discharged from the container.

Inclined planes were most numerous in the hilly Shropshire area, but the Bude Canal had six.

The capacity of boats which could be accommodated on these inclined planes was limited to 5-8 tons; they were commonly known as tub-boats. However, the Blackhill plane on the Monkland Canal could take a boat 70 feet (21 metres) long and 13 feet (4 metres) wide. On the Bude Canal the boats themselves were fitted with wheels to eliminate the need to place them in the wheeled caissons for the journey on the plane.

The Hay inclined plane is scheduled for restoration at the Blists Hill Museum, Ironbridge Gorge, Shropshire. This structure, the design of William Reynolds, operated from 1793 to 1894 to connect the Shropshire and Coalport canals.

One or two pioneer railways were surveyed by canal engineers, who adopted similar principles of construction, that is virtually level stretches connected by a series of short, steep inclined planes. One notable example was the Cromford and High Peak Railway, Derbyshire. This, the first line to cross the Peak District, was designed to link the Peak Forest and Cromford canals. Engineered by Josias Jessop, the 33 mile (53 km) line was opened in 1831, with several noteworthy inclines. Probably the most famous was the Hopton incline, which was worked by a stationary steam engine until 1877, when the line below it was realigned to permit the use of locomotives. Until it closed in 1967, the line was said to be the steepest in Britain worked purely by adhesion, having a gradient of 1 in 14. Another record was set by the incline at Whaley Bridge, which, when it closed in 1952, was the last incline on British Railways operated by a horse-gin. It was the smallest of nine inclines on the railway, with a rise of 40 feet (12 metres) and a gradient of 1 in 13½, and used an endless chain. The engine house at the Middleton Top incline survives, complete with its two 20 horsepower beam engines dating from 1829.

An incline half a mile (0.8 km) long was built on the Leicester and Swannington Railway at Swannington. The winding-engine used to haul wagons from the colliery up the 1 in 17 grade is now preserved at York. Unlike the Middleton Top engine, it is a horizontal machine with a cylinder of 18¼ inches (464 mm) bore.

From 1836 until 1870 trains into Liverpool Lime Street station were hauled by a stationary steam engine and shunted within station limits by horses. Likewise, neighbouring Grand Junction Railway trains were locomotive-hauled to Edge Hill and then worked by stationary engine to the Crown Street station. The first line to serve the Mersey Docks was the Liverpool and Manchester Railway's rope-worked branch from Edge Hill. With improvements in locomotive design and performance, the rope-worked sections were eliminated.

In Manchester, a 1¼ mile (2 km) line was constructed from Victoria Street to Miles Platting, at a ruling grade of 1 in 30. In addition to the stationary winding-engine, trains climbing the incline were often locomotive-assisted. The branch line to Oldham, Lancashire, was built with a gradient of 1 in 27 for nearly half of its 2 mile (3 km) length. This double-track line was operated by locomotive-hauled stock with a balancing train of wagons filled with sand on the adjacent track.

In the early days laden passenger carriages were hauled up and down inclines but, as the operation was not entirely without mishap, from the mid nineteenth century inclines were virtually confined to freight traffic. In 1844 a passenger carriage ran away and was wrecked on the Bagworth incline of the Leicester and Swannington Railway, but it was normal practice for passengers to walk this part of the journey and there were no casual-

The Bowes Railway was one of the best known rope-worked colliery lines in north-east England. Here is shown an empty set of wagons ascending in October 1968.

The rope being detached from a set of wagons at Black Fell Bank on the Bowes Railway.

ties. The Cromford and High Peak line's Sheep Pasture incline was the scene of a spectacular runaway in 1888, when two loaded wagons left the track and shot across the Cromford Canal before coming to rest. As a result of such accidents, run-off points and catch pits were often built to divert and derail runaway vehicles.

Inclines were extensively used in quarrying, often forming part of extensive rail networks within the works. One of the best known systems was at the Dinorwic slate quarries, Llanberis, Gwynedd, where the narrow-gauge inclines remained in use until the quarries closed in the late 1960s. Apart from lowering loaded wagons from the upper levels,

A general view of Morwellham Quay, Devon, in about 1868, in which the inclined plane of the Devon Great Consols Mine can be seen, together with the associated sidings raised on trestles. The Tavistock Canal inclined plane was already beginning to fall into disuse.

Two inclines on the South Hetton Colliery to Seaham Harbour system survived into the 1980s. Here, on the Swines Lodge incline, a set of six loaded wagons starts to descend the three-rail section.

At Hesledon Bank Top, on the Stony Cut incline (the second on the South Hetton Colliery system), a train of loaded wagons waits to depart. This view shows two examples of the false summit, or 'kip'. An ascending rake of wagons would pass over the kip and into a hollow beyond, thus being prevented from rolling back down the incline.

The Swines Lodge brakesman on the South Hetton Colliery system attaches the slip coupling to a train. This featured a quick-release device whereby the brakesman would run alongside the wagons as they rolled to a halt and hit the safety clip with his shunting pole, releasing the coupling. If a mishap occurred he would pull the rapper cord, a wire which ran the full length of the incline. When this was pulled, a weight would drop on to a sheet of tin, alerting his colleagues. By the early 1960s this primitive warning system had been replaced by a telephone.

they were called upon from time to time to lower engines to the workshops for repair.

Docks and harbours were often connected to railways by inclines, although these were frequently replaced in later years by less severely graded lines for locomotive operation. Apart from the first Mersey Docks line already mentioned, examples could be found in the West Country at Newquay, Calstock and Portreath harbours. The Newquay incline, at 1 in 4½, was built largely in tunnel; that at Calstock was replaced by a steam-powered vertical wagon lift. Morwhellham Quay was served by two inclines, one bringing wagons from the Devon Great Consols Mine and the other, worked by a waterwheel, transferring traffic from the Tavistock Canal.

Self-acting inclines were normally double track as, by their nature, a train had to descend at the same time as another ascended. However, to reduce costs, it was possible to use a single line for the lower portion, with a passing loop midway and a double track with common centre rail above.

Above: *An incline preserved at the Dinorwic slate quarries, Llanberis, Gwynedd. Most of the trackwork has disappeared from this once extensive system, although many of the incline structures and winding-houses are still extant.*

Below: *The upper station of the Saltburn Cliff Railway, Cleveland. Water is fed through the apparatus between the tracks into the tanks of the car via the trough on the side panels.*

Saltburn Cliff Railway as seen from the pier in about 1900. At this time the line was of 3 foot 9 inch (1143 mm) gauge; it was rebuilt to standard gauge in 1921.

CLIFF RAILWAYS

The seaside cliff railways are essentially a development of the inclined plane. The first such line was opened at Scarborough, North Yorkshire, in 1875 by the South Cliff Tramway Company. Of standard gauge, it was laid at a gradient of 1 in 1.75 and operated on the water-balance principle. Sea-water was pumped to a reservoir at the top of the cliff, from which it was transferred to tanks under the car at the upper station. After the 284 foot (87 metre) journey the water was returned to the sea and the cycle recommenced with the second car.

Also in north-east England, in Cleveland, the Saltburn Improvement Society built, in 1883, a cliff railway for this developing resort, 207 feet (63 metres) long and with a steady gradient of 1 in 1.33. It was another water-balance installation and, originally laid to 3 foot 9 inch (1143 mm) gauge, it was rebuilt to standard 4 foot 8½ inch (1435 mm) gauge in 1921. The original gas engines have now been replaced by electric motors.

Two years later, in 1885, a funicular was opened at Leas Cliff, Folkestone, Kent. The rails were laid to 5 foot 10 inch (1778 mm) gauge and the cars held eighteen passengers each. As this soon proved too small to cope with traffic demands, two further lines were added in 1890, but this time of a different gauge, 4 feet 10 inches (1473 mm).

The car bodies of the Scarborough, Saltburn and Leas Cliff lines were maintained at all times in a horizontal position, mounted on large triangular underframes to adapt to the gradient. These frames also conveniently housed the water tanks. However, the 1890 cars at Folkestone were of stepped-floor construction, that is tiers of seats across the width of the car were stepped in 'toast-rack' style. Flat-floor cars normally had a door at each end, with longitudinal seats both sides. In the toast-rack-type cars, seat backs were normally reversible so that passengers could face the direction of travel.

Left: *The Devil's Dyke steep-grade railway on the Sussex South Downs worked for only about ten years. The variation in gradient along the line's 840 foot (256 metre) length can be clearly seen.*

Above right: *The South Cliff line in Scarborough, North Yorkshire, was Britain's first cliff railway, opened in July 1875. The present cars, illustrated here, date from 1935.*

Below: *Detail of a car underframe on Scarborough's South Cliff line.*

Right: *The Leas Cliff line in Folkestone, Kent, was first opened in 1885; five years later a second pair of tracks was added. Both sets of tracks were visible in this 1953 view, but today only the lines on the left of the picture are in operation. These cars have a flat-floor design, while the other pair were of stepped-floor construction.*

Another hydraulic line was built in Folkestone in 1904 to serve the Metropole Hotel. It was never rebuilt after a period of disuse during the Second World War and was dismantled in 1951.

At Hastings, East Sussex, the West Hill Lift was opened in 1891. For most of its length it was built in tunnel. Partly using a natural cave, the structure was brick-lined and two 6 foot (1828 mm) gauge tracks were laid for the 500 foot (150 metre) line. A Crossley 40 horse-power gas engine was installed to power a constant-haulage winding-drum and the two cars were run on the same cable system (not independently).

Hastings soon had a second line, the

Below: *The West Hill Lift in Hastings, East Sussex, was opened in 1891. Running largely through tunnel (left), it is today operated by the local authority. At the upper station passengers enter and leave the car by the door at the far end (see detail of the interior, centre). The lower station entrance is illustrated on the right.*

Above: *The East Cliff Lift at Hastings is the steepest of the lines in the south of England, with a gradient of 1 in 1.128. In the foreground can be seen a miniature railway and the fishermen's net shops on the foreshore.*

Left: *The lower terminus of the Hastings East Cliff Lift, opened in 1903.*

East Cliff Lift. Built in 1903, it was promoted by the local authority, unlike its earlier counterpart, although that line too was acquired by the corporation in 1947. The East Cliff line is shorter, at only 267 feet (81 metres), although steeper, at 1 in 1.28. Built by Erith Ironworks, it is a water-balance line, the car tanks each holding 600 gallons (2700 litres). Water is recycled and a storage sump is provided at the lower level; electric pumps raise the water for use.

The publisher Sir George Newnes financed the construction of the Lynmouth and Lynton Cliff Railway in Devon. Designed by George Marks, who was to play a leading role in the design and construction of subsequent funiculars, the Lynmouth line, at 890 feet (271 metres), was the longest cliff railway in

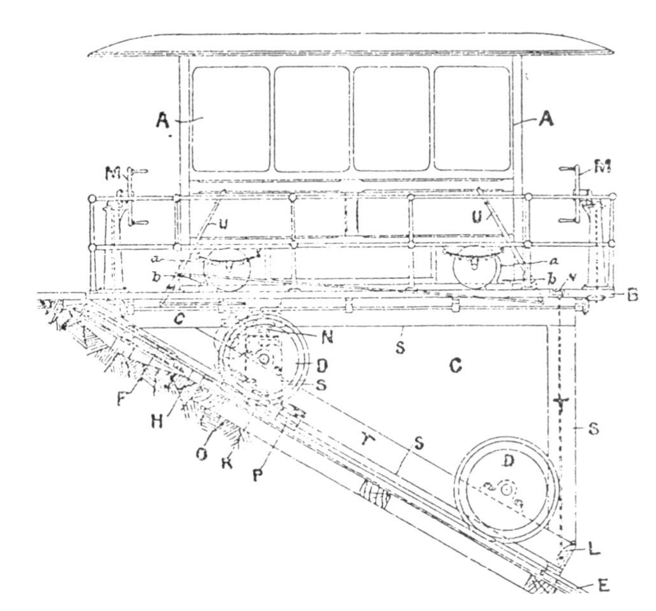

Left: *This drawing by George Marks of a car for the Lynmouth and Lynton Cliff Railway in Devon was attached to his 1888 patent application, which covered, among other things, improvements in automatic braking systems.*

Below: *The lower station at Lynmouth. Note the small wheels which allow the carriage body to be removed so that the undercarriage can be used as a goods platform.*

Britain. A water-balance system, it took water from the river Lyn. An unusual feature of the original cars was that the bodies could be wheeled on and off the undercarriage so that the latter could be used for carrying goods, including motor cars.

George Marks also designed a four-track line, built entirely in tunnel, close to the Clifton Suspension Bridge in Bristol. Opened in 1893, it ran from Hotwells Road to Zion Hill. It was a water-balance system, the water being recycled by pumps powered by an Otto gas engine.

Left: *The top station of the Bridgnorth Castle Hill line, Shropshire, in 1956, when the distinctive car body was still relatively new.*

Right: *Another view of the Bridgnorth line, showing one of the cars built after an accident in 1943. At the same time the motive power was changed to electricity.*

The line closed in 1934 but during the Second World War the tunnel was converted into an emergency studio by the BBC.

Bridgnorth, Shropshire, is a town split into two levels, known as High Town and Low Town, which since 1892 have been connected by the Castle Hill Railway, or 'The Lift'. It rises 118 feet (36 metres) in a length of 200 feet (61 metres) and considerable excavation work through red sandstone was required in the course of its construction. Problems were encountered with the discovery of several caves and with the proximity of existing buildings. The railway was built as a water-balance line but, following an accident in 1943, which occurred during cable changing, killing the manager and wrecking both cars, it was converted to electric

Right: *The electrically driven St Nicholas Lift at Scarborough, North Yorkshire, was opened in 1929. It is 103 feet (31 metres) long, with a steady gradient of 1 in 1.33.*

Below: *The 45 horsepower electric motor which drives the St Nicholas Lift at Scarborough is housed at the upper station. Each car is secured by two ¾ inch (19 mm) steel cables and has a capacity of thirty passengers.*

The two cars on Scarborough's North Bay Lift, dating from 1930, are identical to those of the St Nicholas Lift.

The Central Tramway at Scarborough, opened in 1881, was converted from steam to electric winding-gear in 1920. The line was rebuilt in 1932, when the present cars were supplied.

Messrs Waygood built the 750 foot (230 metre) long Babbacombe Cliff Railway at Torquay, Devon, in 1926.

operation. Metropolitan Vickers supplied the winding-gear and the cars were again rebuilt in 1955. The line is still working and, unlike the other remaining cliff lines, it runs throughout the year.

A short-lived funicular was built to climb the South Downs at Devil's Dyke near Brighton, East Sussex, and opened in 1897. Its winding-drum was powered by a Hornsby-Ackroyd oil engine. However, the anticipated traffic did not materialise and the line survived for only about ten years.

Most cliff lines are built to a uniform constant gradient but the Devil's Dyke line followed the contours of the hillside: the varying grade meant that it could not be operated as a self-acting incline.

The Sandgate funicular near Folkestone was also built with varying gradients, ranging from 1 in 4.75 to 1 in 7.04. However, the two cars were hydraulically operated, but independently, each using a water tank descending a shaft (the principle previously described for the Bude Canal incline).

Scarborough was the site of the United Kingdom's first cliff line but four other lines were subsequently built in the town. Only one no longer survives, the second line, promoted by the Queen's Parade Tramway Company, which worked only from 1879 until 1887, when a major landslip forced its closure. The ill-fated venture had already suffered a runaway car — even before the line had opened. The Central Tramway, opened in 1881, proved more successful. It utilised a steam winding-engine and the track was of standard gauge, with a separate channel between the rails for an emergency screw brake. Scarborough Corporation operates the town's other two lifts, the St Nicholas and North Cliff lifts, dating from 1929 and 1930 respectively. Both were built for electric operation: the two earlier lines have now been modernised with similar mechanisms. The St Nicholas line has a gauge of 7 feet 6 inches (2286 mm) at a gradient of 1 in 1.33. The North Cliff Lift has identical cars but is laid to a 6 foot 6 inch (1981 mm) gauge.

Not all proposals for cliff lines came to fruition. At Ventnor, on the Isle of Wight's hilly southern coast, a series of schemes was put forward between 1889

Aberystwyth, Dyfed, now has the only cliff railway in Britain to use stepped carriages. The gradient of the line varies to assist with acceleration and deceleration of the cars, one of the features patented by George Marks in 1895.

The lower station of the Aberystwyth line in 1957. The fare of 6d was cheaper than when the line opened in 1896!

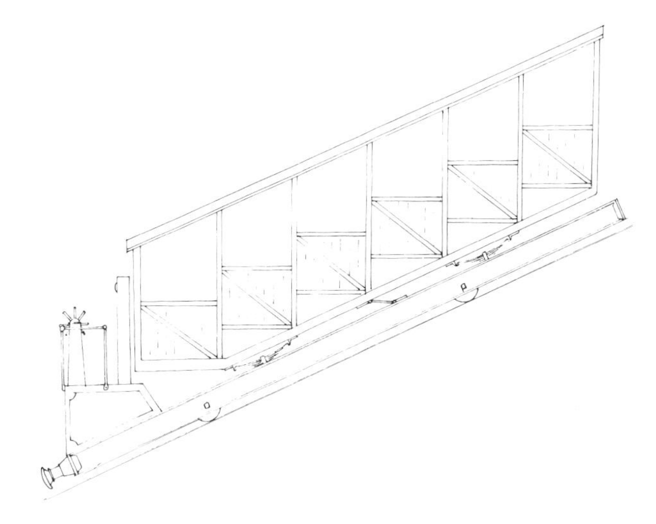

Left: *The two cars for the Aberystwyth line were built locally by R. Jones and Son. The original water-balance mechanism was replaced by an electric winding system in 1921, when the 1000 gallon (4500 litre) water tank mounted on the lower platform end of each car was removed.*

Below left: *The Falcon Cliff Lift was built to serve the hotel of that name at Douglas, Isle of Man. Although the first lift was built in 1887, the present installation dates from 1927.*

Below right: *The Isle of Man's second funicular line was at Douglas Head. By 1947 it was closed, but still intact.*

Bournemouth, Dorset, has three lifts. This view shows one of the original cars on the East Cliff line in 1948.

and 1924 to link the town with its railway station, some 270 feet (82 metres) above sea level. Some of the proposals went further, with planned extensions to the Esplanade below and upwards to Littleton Downs. The line projected in 1898 by the Ventnor Inclined Light Railway Company envisaged a 5 foot 9 inch (1753 mm) gauge line, rising 598 feet (182 metres), worked in three sections with two cars to each. Although two sections of line were authorised in 1899, it was never built. Much more recently, in 1961, a cable tramway was proposed from Great Malvern to the top of the Worcestershire Beacon, nearly 1400 feet (427 metres) high, but the idea was abandoned in favour of a chair lift.

At Douglas, Isle of Man, an inclined railway was built in 1887 to link the promenade with the Falcon Cliff Hotel. This was dismantled a few years later and re-erected at Port Soderick, where it ran until 1939. A new line was built at Falcon Cliff in 1927 by Wadsworth, the Bolton lift manufacturer. A single track of 5 foot (1524 mm) gauge with one car, it is electrically operated. It used a 400 volt direct current supply until 1950, when it changed to 415 volt three-phase alternating current. Another funicular, the Douglas Head Inclined Railway, operated nearby.

All cliff railways incorporate a number of safety features. Normally a governor automatically stops the machinery if the cars exceed their predetermined speed and, in the event of the cable breaking or tension slackening, an automatic brake acts on each car to secure it to the track. In addition, the conductor (if carried) would have a hand-operated emergency brake.

George Marks patented several safety devices, including the automatic brake, which stopped cars by means of steel wedges on the running rails, and a centrifugal governor on the car axle. He also designed a hydraulic brake system which utilised water pressure (up to 1000 pounds per square inch, or 70 kg per square centimetre) to keep the brakes off: a 'fail-safe' system. The car conductor was also required to maintain a hold on the operating handle during the journey, as premature release would also cause the brake to be applied. This was the precursor of the 'dead man's handle' now used on main-line railways. Normally car and station doors are interlocked for safety and a bell signalling system is installed between the winding-house and the cars.

Many of the surviving cliff lines have been rebuilt over the years, often converted to electric traction, and they continue to provide a useful transport function.

EUROPEAN LINES

Funicular lines were also built in other, mountainous regions of Europe: about 25 were in operation at the outbreak of the First World War.

A steam funicular was built on the slopes of Mount Vesuvius in 1880, while

Above: *By 1964 Bournemouth's attractive clerestory-roofed cars had been replaced by the two more modern vehicles shown here on the East Cliff line.*

Left: *An identical car on the West Cliff line. All the Bournemouth lines, electrically driven, are operated by the local authority.*

The single-track line at Southend, Essex, photographed while closed for the winter in February 1952.

an electrically driven example was constructed at Leopoldsberg near Vienna five years later.

George Marks constructed a water-balance scheme in Budapest. The line, opened in 1896, ascended from the banks of the river Danube to the Blocksberg fortress above the city.

Three funicular lines were built in Barcelona. The first, dating from 1901, climbs to a pleasure park at Tibidabo and uses two-car sets dating from 1958. In 1906 the city's second line was opened at Vallividera and in 1931 the Montjuich mountain line was added. This last line is operated in two sections: the lower section uses two-car trains and is mostly in tunnel, while the upper section, to the twelfth-century castle, overlooks the port area.

Several funicular lines were constructed in Portugal. In the Minho region, a line was operated from Viana do Castelo by the main-line railway company. A line was built in 1882 at Braga, with a Riggenbach centre rack rail for use as an emergency brake. The double-track line was of standard gauge and worked on the water-balance principle, using Swiss-built cars. Porto, which still has an interesting tramway system, has now lost its funicular line, which was built in 1889. Three such lines have been operated in Lisbon. One of these, the Lavra line, was built in 1884; the cars themselves are equipped with electric traction motors taking current from overhead wires, although they are connected by cable and work together as a counterbalanced system. All three Lisbon lines were either built as, or later converted to, 3 foot (900 mm) gauge.

In southern France the Aven Armand funicular railway, which was built in 1926 entirely in tunnel, has eight-wheeled cars each carrying forty passengers. It uses rubber-tyred cars. (A similar idea has been adopted on part of the Paris Metro system.) In Paris a funicular was built at Montmartre for the World's Fair in 1900, originally having a centre rack rail for use as an emergency brake.

One notable Swiss funicular is the Parsenn railway, which climbs 3630 feet (1110 metres) from Davros to Weissfluhjoch over a distance of 2 miles (3 km). It is particularly unusual as it uses cars coupled in pairs, with a combined capacity of 140 passengers.

The steepest funicular in the world is

A car arriving at the upper station of the Bom Jesus funicular at Braga in Portugal. Note the centre rack rail for emergency braking.

Many European funiculars were built as single lines with a central passing loop; a high proportion used cars with stepped bodies, as typified by this French example. In order to eliminate the need for conventional points at the passing loop, some lines used cars with double-flanged wheels on one side of each axle, and without flanges on the other, to guide the cars correctly as they passed.

another Swiss line, running between Piotta and Piora in Canton Ticino, with a gradient of 1 in 1.125. Operated by a single car, it was built to transport materials to a hydro-electric scheme construction site and later adapted for passenger operation. Another spectacular Swiss line runs from Schlatti to Stoos, crossing the Muota river in its 0.9 mile (1.4 km) length. The line from Sierra in the Rhone valley is used to carry freight up to the mountain resort of Montana-Vermala. The passenger cars each have a small goods wagon attached, into which cargo is loaded in cages. The Sierra-Montana line also has the longest single cable length of the Swiss lines, although the complete railway is operated in two sections with a total length of 2.6 miles (4.2 km).

While most of the Swiss lines are now electrically operated, a few examples, such as the relatively short Territet-Glion line, retain the water-balance system. One other line, which ran from Ouchy (Lake Geneva) to Lausanne, used water turbines but was converted from the funicular principle to a rack and pinion

Above: *The Lavra line in Lisbon. Unusually, the overhead wires supply current to traction motors on the cars, although they are both connected by cable.*

Below: *The Montmartre line in Paris was built for the World's Fair in 1900. It was also originally equipped with a rack rail for braking, although this was later dispensed with.*

system in 1959. In its funicular days it often ran three- or even four-coach trains, an unusual occurrence on this type of railway. Two funiculars run from Interlaken, one of which, the Harder Railway, offers superb views as it climbs to the Brienzen Grat. The resort of Giessbach is approached by a funicular from Lake Brienz.

CABLE TRAMWAYS

The concept of cable haulage has not been confined to relatively short cliff railways and inclined planes. In the nineteenth century a number of tramway systems were built using cable traction, not always because the routes were severely graded.

The first such tramway in the United Kingdom was the Highgate Hill Cable Tramway, London, opened in May 1884, although cable traction had been used on the London and Blackwall Railway in the 1840s. The Highgate Hill line was built to 3 foot 6 inch (1067 mm) gauge and was subject to a maximum gradient of 1 in 11.

However, a decade earlier, Andrew Hallidie, a Californian wire-rope manufacturer, saw the possibilities for a cable tramway in San Francisco; this was opened in 1873. The now famous cable-cars still operate on Clay Street Hill.

Edinburgh Northern Tramways adopted the principle to overcome the problem of traversing the steep gradient between Princes Street and Queen Street, using a 1300 horsepower winding-engine. So successful was this scheme that Edinburgh Corporation decided to follow suit with its own. Soon after 1900 Edinburgh had a fleet of 205 double-deck cable-cars operating on 36 miles (58 km) of track but by 1922 the system was converted to electric tramcars with conventional 'trolley' current collection.

The Handsworth area of Birmingham also had a cable tramway. Although originally horse-drawn and of standard gauge, it was relaid to 3 foot 6 inch (1067 mm) gauge when converted to cable traction in 1888. Cable operation sur-

City of Birmingham cable-car number 96, on the Handsworth route at Thornhill Road, about 1909.

The Llandudno station of the Great Orme Tramway in Gwynedd. This is the only British line operated in two sections, necessitating a change of car at the halfway point.

Detailed view of a point at the passing loop of the upper section of the Great Orme line. Cables pass through frogs in the running rails.

Left: *The cable position of the Great Orme line is maintained on curves by the frequent use of sheaves and pulleys.*

Right: *On the lower section of the Great Orme line the cable is enclosed in conduit. The cast iron covers allow access to the pulleys beneath for lubrication. Note the wooden protective cover at the conduit junction slot, which is put in position each night after the last car has passed.*

vived here until 1911. One of the cable-cars has been rescued for preservation by the Black Country Museum at Dudley, West Midlands.

George Marks, of cliff railway fame, engineered the Matlock Steep Incline Tramway in Derbyshire with W. N. Colson, who had been engineer for the Edinburgh and Birmingham cable systems. Half a mile (0.8 km) long, the line was built with gradients up to a maximum of 1 in 5. It was single-track with a midway passing loop. Two stationary steam engines drove the endless cable at a steady 6 mph (10 km/h). Despite the severe gradients, the cars used 'grippers' to gain traction. Opened in 1893, the line was never a great financial success and closed in 1927. Another inclined tramway engineered by Marks was the also unsuccessful Swansea Constitution Hill line. This short line, built in 1897, at first failed to satisfy the Board of Trade on safety grounds and, after modifications, ran for only four years.

Unlike cars on cliff lines, cable tramway vehicles were not permanently attached to the haulage cable. Instead, a 'gripper' was installed on each vehicle which would grip the endless, constantly moving cable. The first gripper system had been patented by Curtis in 1838.

The cable was laid in a separate conduit between the running rails, with a groove for the gripper to pass through. The cable was supported on sheaves or pulleys but with additional vertical pulleys at regular intervals to guide the cable around curves, keeping it taut and in the centre of the conduit.

The cables were wound by separate power houses. The maximum cable length of any British system was 6½ miles (10.5 km), in Edinburgh. Each cable was diverted at some point to the engine house. At points and junctions between cables it was necessary for the driver or brakesman to detach the gripper and

The little Shipley Glen Tramway, near Bradford, West Yorkshire, built in 1895, originally used cars designed for a fairground ride. The present vehicles date from 1956.

The Shipley Glen Tramway uses two pairs of open toast-rack cars, each pair permanently coupled. Note the reversible seat backs.

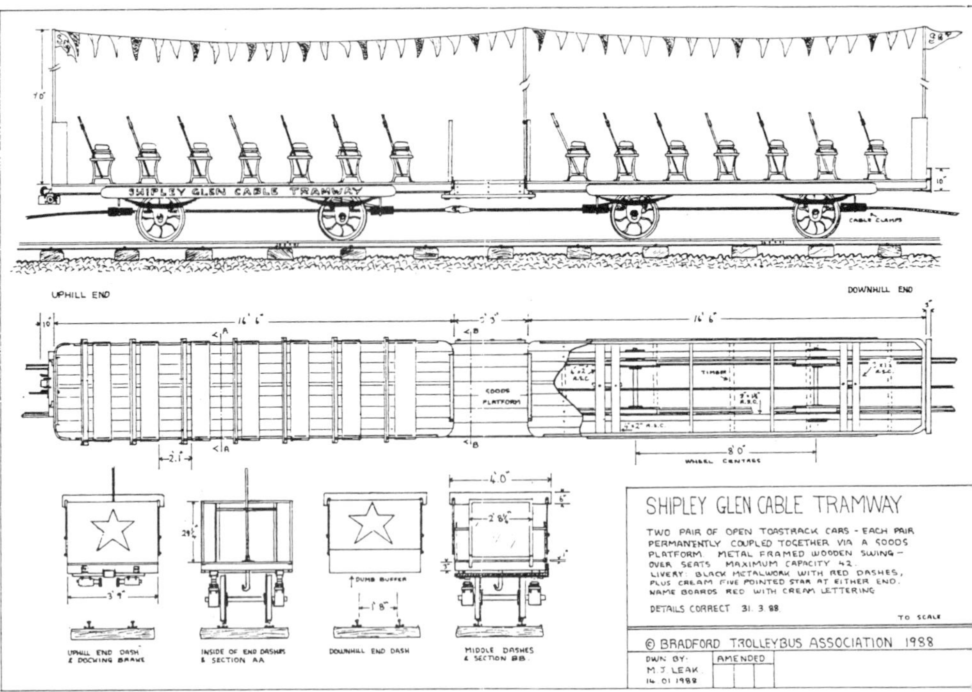

'freewheel' over the joint, until he could grip the next cable.

The cable tramways were not altogether successful; in their later years the Edinburgh and Birmingham systems were the victims of frequent breakdowns. Cables occasionally broke completely or, as they wore, strands would become detached and entangled with the car gripper mechanisms. In the latter case the car could not be stopped and there was no easy and direct communication with the winding-house. Whenever a cable had to be stopped, all the cars using it would also be delayed. Other problems included obstructions in the conduit, pulley failure and the risk of stranding at junctions. In addition, cable track was more expensive both to install and maintain.

One fine example of a cable tramway system still in operation is the Great Orme Tramway, Llandudno, Gwynedd, which runs from the town to the summit of the headland from which it takes its name, nearly 700 feet (215 metres) above sea level. It was built in two sections, with the winding-house for both parts at the halfway point. The lower section is the steeper part of the line and is laid out as a street tramway, with the cable enclosed in conduit, while on the upper section the cables are exposed.

The pier railway at Southport, Merseyside, opened in 1860 with a length of 0.8 mile (1.3 km), was the first pier line to be built and the second longest. From 1863 to 1905 it was cable-operated. The Glasgow District Subway was cable-operated from its opening in 1897 until 1935.

At Llechwedd Slate Caverns, Gwynedd, a short funicular conveys visitors into the mine.

FURTHER READING

Allen, Cecil J. *Switzerland's Amazing Railways*. Nelson, third edition 1965.
Anderson, R.C. *Great Orme Railway*. Light Railway Transport League.
Hadfield, Charles. *British Canals, An Illustrated History*. David and Charles, seventh edition 1984.
Hart, Brian. *Folkestone's Cliff Lifts*. Millgate Publishing, 1985.
Lane, Michael. *Baron Marks of Woolwich*. Quiller Press, 1987.

Modern Tramway is a monthly journal published jointly by Ian Allan and the Light Railway Transport League. It features occasional articles and news items regarding funicular lines. In addition, many of the cliff railways listed under 'Places to visit' publish their own souvenir guide books.

PLACES TO VISIT

Aberystwyth Cliff Railway, Cliff Terrace, Aberystwyth, Dyfed. Telephone: 0970 617642.
Babbacombe Cliff Lift, Babbacombe, Torquay, Devon.
Birmingham Museum of Science and Industry, Newhall Street, Birmingham B3 1RZ. Telephone: 021-236 1022.
Blists Hill Open Air Museum, Legges Way, Madeley, Telford, Shropshire. Telephone: 0952 586063, 583003 or 586309.
Bournemouth: East Cliff Lift, Undercliff Drive; *West Cliff Lift*, West Promenade; *Southbourne Lift*, Pokesdown.
Bowes Railway, Springwell Village, Gateshead, Tyne and Wear NE9 7QJ. Telephone: 091-416 1847.
Bridgnorth Castle Hill Railway, 6a Castle Terrace, Bridgnorth, Shropshire. Telephone: 07462 2052.
Broadstairs Lift, 13 Belmont Road, Broadstairs, Kent.
Exeter Maritime Museum, The Haven, Exeter, Devon EX8 8DT. Telephone: 0392 58075.
Folkestone: Leas Cliff Lift, The Leas, Folkestone, Kent.
Great Orme Tramway, Victoria Street, Llandudno, Gwynedd.
Hastings: East Cliff Lift, Rock-a-Nore; *West Hill Lift*, George Street.
Lynmouth and Lynton Cliff Lift, The Esplanade, Lynmouth, Devon.
Middleton Top Engine House, Rise End, Wirksworth, Derbyshire. Telephone: 062982 3204.
Morwellham Quay Open Air Museum, Morwellham, Tavistock, Devon PL19 8JL. Telephone: 0822 832766.
Saltburn Cliff Lift, Saltburn, Cleveland.
Scarborough: South Cliff Tramway; Central Tramway; St Nicholas Lift; North Cliff Lift.
Shipley Glen Tramway, Prod Lane, Baildon, Bradford, West Yorkshire. Telephone: 0274 589010. Operated by Bradford Trolleybus Association.
Southend Cliff Lift, Cliff Hill, Southend, Essex.
Welsh Slate Museum, Gilfach Ddu, Llanberis, Gwynedd LL55 4TY. Telephone: 0286 870630.